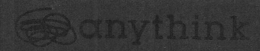

PUBLISHED BY CREATIVE EDUCATION AND CREATIVE PAPERBACKS
P.O. BOX 227, MANKATO, MINNESOTA 56002
CREATIVE EDUCATION AND CREATIVE PAPERBACKS
ARE IMPRINTS OF THE CREATIVE COMPANY
WWW.THECREATIVECOMPANY.US

DESIGN AND PRODUCTION BY CHRISTINE VANDERBEEK
ART DIRECTION BY RITA MARSHALL
PRINTED IN THE UNITED STATES OF AMERICA

PHOTOGRAPHS BY ALAMY (IMAGE SOURCE SALSA, JOHNER IMAGES,
NORDICPHOTOS), CORBIS (HERO IMAGES INC.), GETTY IMAGES (JOHN KUCZALA),
ISTOCKPHOTO (13460889, CASEYHILLPHOTO, MOLOKO88, TMARVIN),
SHUTTERSTOCK (AJT, DENISNATA, GORILLAIMAGES, DEREK HATFIELD, BOGDAN
IONESCU, WEERACHAI KHAMFU, KOKHANCHIKOV, KRASOWIT, BRUCE MACQUEEN,
ROCKSWEEPER, SEKTOR, LJUPCO SMOKOVSKI, PAN XUNBIN)

LIBRARY OF CONGRESS CATALOGING-IN-PUBLICATION DATA
ROSEN, MICHAEL J.
TACKLING THE BOX / MICHAEL J. ROSEN.
P. CM. — (REEL TIME)
INCLUDES INDEX.
SUMMARY: A PRIMER ON THE BASIC DOS AND DON'TS OF FISHING, INCLUDING TIPS
ON ORGANIZING A TACKLE BOX, ADVICE ON HOW TO SELECT HOOKS AND BAIT,
AND INSTRUCTIONS FOR MAKING A HANDLINE.

ISBN 978-1-60818-776-8 (HARDCOVER)
ISBN 978-1-62832-384-9 (PBK)
ISBN 978-1-56660-818-3 (EBOOK)
THIS TITLE HAS BEEN SUBMITTED FOR CIP PROCESSING UNDER LCCN 2016010305.

CCSS: RI.3.1, 2, 3, 4, 5, 7, 8, 10; RI.4.1, 2, 3, 4, 7, 10; RI.5.1, 2, 4, 10;
RF.3.3, 4; RF.4.3, 4; RF.5.3, 4

FIRST EDITION HC 9 8 7 6 5 4 3 2 1
FIRST EDITION PBK 9 8 7 6 5 4 3 2 1

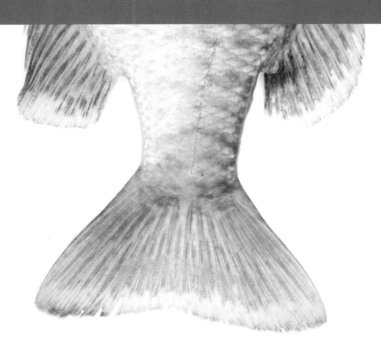

TACKLING THE BOX

→ MICHAEL J. ROSEN ←

CREATIVE EDUCATION ⚓ CREATIVE PAPERBACKS

TABLE OF CONTENTS

HOOK, LINE, AND SINKER

The sections of a tackle box can help keep your fishing gear organized and easy to find.

Fishing season is about to begin. As you prepare, you look over your checklist. This is the best time to sort your trusty tackle box. Time to get to work! Tackle boxes help keep fishing gear organized. You can buy a tackle box at a sporting goods store. Or you can find something around your home that's lightweight, durable, and unlikely to rust. A plastic lunchbox or sewing box would work well. A small travel bag might also do the trick.

You'll need smaller containers to hold individual pieces of tackle. Gather small boxes or jars. Empty plastic medicine bottles or spice jars are just the right size. An empty spool or craft stick is great for winding extra fishing line.

In your box, you will need bait or lures to attract fish. You will need hooks to catch hold of fish. And you will need a lightweight line to put the bait and hook where fish will see it.

But wait! You'll need one more thing that won't fit inside a tackle box. A pole, rod, or stick to hold on to the line will have to be carried.

Depending on what you are trying to catch, you may also need to bring a small net.

HOOKED!

Try not to handle live bait too much, as your skin carries a scent that fish can smell.

lways be careful around hooks. A hook is sharp enough to pierce a fish's tough lip. That means it's sharp enough to poke you, too! In your tackle box, keep hooks inside another container. If you're fishing with a handline or pole, sink the hook in a piece of cork. With a rod and reel, slip your hook into one of the rod's guides. Reel in the line to hold the hook in place.

For catch-and-release fishing, try using a barbless hook. You can make one from any regular hook. Use pliers to squeeze the barb down. This will make the hook into a simple "J." The "J" will hook a fish, but it won't plant itself a second time inside the fish's lip. This makes releasing the fish much easier. Keep

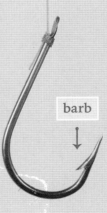

barb

your line tight as you play the fish. It will
stay hooked, even without the barb.

You should have a few hooks of
different sizes. That way, if you need to cut
one loose in a snag, you'll have a spare. Or,
if you find that bigger or smaller fish are
biting, you can switch to the right size!

Even in water that looks obstacle-free, your hook could get stuck.

THE RIGHT BAIT

Always bait your hook for the kind of fish that are biting. Many kinds of fish like nightcrawlers. You can buy them at a tackle shop or sporting goods store. Or you can "farm" your own!

Simply wet a patch of grass for a couple nights in a row. Then, after dark, collect your bait. Cover a flashlight with red or yellow tissue paper or plastic wrap. Shine it on the damp grass. A nightcrawler keeps its tail buried. When startled, it will quickly retreat underground. Quick! Grab the worm before it disappears!

Keep your worms in a lidded container. Moss, dirt, or dead leaves make the best bedding. The bedding should be damp. But don't use tap water to wet it down! Use fresh water instead. To store worms for a day or two, put them in a cooler with bags of ice.

Bass and catfish want a big mouthful of bait. When these fish are biting, you'll want to use a larger hook. Try a #1 or #0 hook. "Gob" two or three worms on the hook. Poke the hook two or three times through each worm.

Smaller fish, such as bluegills and crappies (*CROP-eez*), need a smaller hook. Try using a #6 hook and a single worm. Insert the hook's point into the middle of the worm. Slide it along until most of the hook is buried in the worm.

On the eastern shore, you can catch bluefish in 6 to 20 feet (1.8–6.1 m) of water.

Some fish prefer different bait. Minnows, doughballs, and lures are a few other types of bait you can try. Research what works best for fish in your area. Be sure to bring along lots of bait when you go fishing!

LINES AND POLES

Make your own handline using a slim tree branch, and tie on some fishing line.

You don't have to own a rod and reel to enjoy fishing. A handline is a "fishing pole" without the pole. It's just a strong, smooth stick with a hook, sinker, and bobber. A broken broom handle, a tree branch, or any stick that's at least six inches (15.2 cm) long would work.

Or you could attach the line to a longer pole. Even without a reel, a pole can place bait farther out in the water. A pole should be stiff and strong, but bendable. It should be five to six feet (1.5–1.8 m) long. The best pole will be one inch (2.5 cm) thick at the bottom and narrow to half an inch (0.3 cm) at the tip. Look for oak, hickory, hazel, willow, or ash tree branches.

These woods are both strong and flexible. Don't cut a live limb from a tree! Use a fallen or recently dead branch. Avoid rotten, weak, or cracked branches. Strip off any twigs and leaves and cut a small notch around the tip of the pole. (This will keep your line from sliding off.) Then tie on about six feet (1.8 m) of line. Prepare your line and bait your hook.

When you hook a fish with your handline, lift the tip of your pole and pull it toward you. Grab the line. Lead the fish to shallow water. Use a net to land it. Gently remove the barbless hook and return the fish to the water.

Success! Now, bait up and try again!

Ice fishing calls for different equipment and methods to catch slower-moving fish.

ACTIVITY: ASSEMBLING YOUR HANDLINE

HANDLINES ARE INEXPENSIVE, RELIABLE, AND EASY TO ASSEMBLE. YOU CAN MAKE YOUR OWN FROM RECYCLED MATERIALS.

MATERIALS

- 6 to 7 feet (1.8–2.1 m) of fishing line
- a smooth, straight stick
- a #6 hook
- split-shot sinkers
- pliers
- a wine cork or empty thread spool

1 Attach the fishing line to the stick with a tight double knot. Make the knot about two inches (5.1 cm) from the end of the stick. Cut a notch above the knot to keep the line from slipping off.

2 Add a bobber. Use a piece of cork with a hole drilled through it. Or use a small, empty spool. Thread the line through the center of the bobber and tie it in place—about as far up from the end of the line as the water is deep.

3 Attach a #6 hook to the end of the line with a *clinch knot.*

4 Add a *split-shot sinker* about 10 inches (25.4 cm) above the hook. Slide the fishing line between the sinker's two halves. Squeeze the halves together with pliers. Use two sinkers in a stronger *current* to keep the bait underwater.

5 Bait your hook. You are ready to fish!

bobber → a small, floating object used to keep the hook at a certain depth

clinch knot → a widely used fishing knot that secures a fishing line to gear

current → the direction in which a body of water is moving

lures → types of bait someone makes, not natural ones such as flies, worms, or other animals

split-shot sinker → a small weight used to help a baited hook sink; the line is threaded into the opening of a split-shot sinker

tackle → gear used in fishing, such as hooks, sinkers, bobbers, and bait

READ MORE

Bourne, Wade. *The Pocket Fishing Basics Guide: Freshwater Basics, Hook, Line & Sinker*. New York: Skyhorse, 2012.

Parker, Steve. *Fish*. New York: DK, 2005.

WEBSITES

Fishing Tips Depot

http://www.fishingtipsdepot.com/

Find fishing tips by species, technique, and type.

Take Me Fishing: How to Fish

http://www.takemefishing.org/how-to-fish/

Learn more about fishing, and find places to fish near you!

Note: Every effort has been made to ensure that the websites listed above are suitable for children, that they have educational value, and that they contain no inappropriate material. However, because of the nature of the Internet, it is impossible to guarantee that these sites will remain active indefinitely or that their contents will not be altered.

INDEX